jonah, micah and nahum

the books of

jonah

micah and nahum

authorised king james version

printed by authority

published by canongate

with an introduction by | alasdair gray

First published in Great Britain in 1999
by Canongate Books Ltd
14 High Street, Edinburgh EH1 1TE

10 9 8 7 6 5 4 3 2 1

Introduction copyright © Alasdair Gray 1999
The moral right of the author has been asserted

Extract from *On the Mass Bombing of Iraq and Kuwait, Commonly Known as
'The Gulf War'* © Tom Leonard 1991

British Library Cataloguing-in-Publication Data
A catalogue record is available on request from
the British Library

ISBN 0 86241 971 9

Typeset by Palimpsest Book Production
Book design by Paddy Cramsie at et al
Printed and bound in Great Britain
by Caledonian International, Bishopbriggs

a note about pocket canons

The Authorised King James Version of the Bible, translated between 1603–11, coincided with an extraordinary flowering of English literature. This version, more than any other, and possibly more than any other work in history, has had an influence in shaping the language we speak and write today.

Twenty-four of the eighty original books of the King James Bible are brought to you in this series. They encompass categories as diverse as history, philosophy, law, poetry and fiction. Each Pocket Canon also has its own introduction, specially commissioned from an impressive range of writers, to provide a personal interpretation of the text and explore its contemporary relevance.

introduction by alasdair gray

*Alasdair Gray is an old asthmatic Glaswegian who lives by paint-
ing, writing and book design. His books are the novels* Lanark,
1982 Janine, The Fall of Kelvin Walker, Something Leather,
McGrotty and Ludmilla, Poor Things, A History Maker; *short
story collections* Unlikely Stories Mostly, Lean Tales *(with
Agnes Owens and James Kelman),* Ten Tales Tall & True,
Mavis Belfrage; *poetry* Old Negatives; *polemic* Why Scots
Should Rule Scotland 1992, Why Scots should Rule Scotland
1997; *play* Working Legs (for people without them); *autobiog-
raphy* Saltire Self Portrait 4; *literary history* The Anthology of
Prefaces. *His hobbies are socialism and liking the English.*

The thirty-nine books called *The Old Testament* in the King
James Bible show the state of the Jews between 900 and 100
BC and preserve legends from more ancient times. They were
edited into their present form by scholars defending their
culture from an empire ruling the place where they lived: an
empire of people equally clever and literate: Greeks whose
books were as various as their gods. Jews were then unique
in worshipping a single God: their folklore, laws, politics
and poetry kept mentioning him. The editors arranged
these books in the chronological order of the subject matter,

producing a story of their people from prehistoric times and making their God the strongest character in world fiction. It began with a second-century BC poem telling how he made the universe and people like a poet, out of words, followed by a fifth-century BC tale of how he made man like a potter, out of clay. It then showed God adapting to his worshippers from prehistoric times to their own.

Adam, Cain and Noah find God punitive but soothed by the smell of burnt flesh, mostly animal. He connives with the tricks of Abraham and Isaac, polygamous nomads who get cattle or revenge by prostituting a wife or cheating foreigners and relatives. When Moses leads Jewish tribes out of Egypt God commands them like a Pharaoh, promising unlimited protection for unlimited obedience. He is a war god when they invade Palestine, smiting them with plague when they do not kill every man, woman, child and animal in a captured city. Their leaders (called prophets because God tells them the future) are fathers of tribal families and military commanders until they get land and cities of their own where (as in other lands) wealth is managed by official landlords and priests who exploit the poor. New kinds of prophet then arise: poets inspired by moral rage who speak for the exploited. They say that if Jewish rulers don't obey God by being just and merciful he will use the might of foreigners to smash their new-made kingdoms. That happens. From 680 BC to 1948 Jews are ruled by foreign empires, first Assyrian and at last British. They outlive so many empires that Norwegian Ibsen calls them the aristocrats of world history, for they can survive without a land and government.

That was not wholly true. They were governed by the words of their prophets, especially those in the last *Old Testament* books who said the Jewish God is also God of all people, even people who oppress them; that God has created Jews to keep his words alive until the whole world learns justice and mercy by obeying him; that before then Jews should welcome suffering as punishment for sin or tests of faith. After the first destruction of Jerusalem in 586 BC this must have sounded a new policy to those who wanted to repossess a national territory gained (as all nations have gained territory) by killing folk. No wonder many Jews assimilated with foreigners and the faithful sometimes sang psalms begging God to leave them alone.

The book of *Jonah* is a prose comedy about a Jew who wants God to leave him alone and cannot grasp that God's policy is now for those of every nation.

Jonah is an unwilling prophet. His Jewish conscience orders him to denounce the wicked Assyrian empire in its capital city so he at once sails towards a different city where he hopes foreign gods will prevail over his own. This breaks the first of the ten commandments: *You shall have no other God than me* (*Deuteronomy* 5): hence the tempest. The international crew see it is aimed at someone aboard. Many verses describe their reluctance to fling Jonah out, even when he tells them it is the one way to save themselves. The book is insisting that mercy is not just a Jewish virtue; but out Jonah goes and God saves him in the belly of a fish. Here the prophet chants a psalm saying God can save those who cry unto him from the belly of hell. This hell is not the eternal torture chamber later adopted by official Christianity. For Jews hell is the worst that living people can suffer and Jonah IS suffering it, unless the fish intestines are a cosy place. But now he knows that God is always with him and he need not fear death.

Then comes a parody of *Exodus*, Chapter 11, perhaps the cruellest book in the *Old Testament*. In it the God of Moses sends Pharaoh a message then hardens Pharaoh's heart to reject it, giving Moses an excuse to condemn all Egyptian first-born children and cattle to death by plague. But God uses Jonah to send the Assyrians a message that softens their king's heart. The king leads his people into abandoning their evil ways, so *God repented of the evil that he had said that he would do unto them; and he did it not* (Jonah 3:10). This contradicts the Mosaic code, which says evil MUST be rewarded with evil.

So Jonah learns he is not a scourge in the hand of God, like Moses, Joshua and Samson, but a reformer, and like many reformers he now looks stupid. It is obvious that the enemy king who thought his people might be persuaded to deserve mercy knew more about God than God's Hebrew prophet. Jonah's short but influential career ends not with a bang but with his dismal whimper: *I knew that thou art a gracious God, and merciful, … Therefore now, O Lord, take, I beseech thee, my life from me, for it is better for me to die than to live* (*Jonah* 4:2–3). God cuts this self-pitying cackle with a short question: *Doest thou well to be angry?* (*Jonah* 4:4) Jonah is too cowardly or childish to admit anger and squats outside the city determined to die by sunstroke if the promise of destruction is not fulfilled. Not even the mercy of miraculous shade cast over him softens this determination. The shade is withdrawn. In a fever Jonah hears God repeat something like his last question. He now answers truthfully and is favoured by words framed like another question. They suggest reasons for both God's action and his inaction: most evil is caused by folly; widespread slaughter is not the best cure if a warning of disaster helps folk to change their ways. We are not told if Jonah learns these lessons because they are meant for *us*.

Believers and unbelievers have argued pointlessly about the truth of Jonah's book because they did not know great truths can be told in fantasies. It was known by editors who put *Jonah* before *Micah* and *Nahum*, realistic books about the destruction of Jerusalem and Nineveh.

Micah starts a prophetic sermon in verse by denouncing the Jews who live in Samaria: God has let Assyria enslave them for disobeying him; soon the princes and priests of Jerusalem will be conquered too, for they seek wealth and luxury instead of justice and mercy, oppressing the poor of their own nation while thinking God's forgiveness can be bought by animal sacrifices. Micah foretells a disastrous but not hopeless future: after much warfare the whole world will find peace by accepting the one true God, for a Jewish ruler from the little town of Bethlehem will become lord of every nation. This prophecy must have inspired hope and dread in every imaginative child born afterwards in Bethlehem.

Nahum came eighty years later. He was probably an

Assyrian slave when all Jewish territory had been conquered as Micah foretold. Nahum saw the destruction of Nineveh by the combined armies of Babylon and Persia: these killed and enslaved the people and washed the city away by channelling the River Tigris into it. The only grand truth in Nahum's triumphant song is that nations who keep living by armaments will perish by them. Most governments, including the British, think this only true of foreign nations. I quote from Tom Leonard's *On the Mass Bombing of Iraq and Kuwait, Commonly Known as 'The Gulf War' with Leonard's Shorter Catechism.* AK Press published it in 1991.

Q. What did Britain take part in on Tuesday, February 19, 1991?

A. It took part in what was at that point 'one of the most ferocious attacks on the centre of Baghdad', using bombers and Cruise missiles fired from ships.

Q. What did John Major say about the bombing the next day?

A. He said: 'One is bound to ask about attacks such as these: what sort of people is it that can carry them out? They certainly are consumed with hate. They are certainly sick of mind, and they can be certain of one thing – they will be hunted and hunted until they are found.'

(He was talking about 5 lb of explosive left in a litter basket at Victoria Station in London. This killed one person and critically injured three.)

Major's government contained people privately enriched by weapon sales to both Britain's army and the army of the dictator we fought. We fought him again before Christmas 1998 when our most highly respected newspapers said that, though wicked and undemocratic, this dictator had better stay in power to stop Iraq falling apart and increasing the cost of our petrol. Meanwhile, since our troops in 1991 fired bullets tipped with uranium, babies are now being born in Iraq with distorted bodies and heads, others without heads.

When a child, Ernest Levy lost faith in a purely national god by living through Auschwitz and Belsen. He became a cantor in a Glasgow synagogue and now believes God is the innocent, creative, spiritual part of everyone. This sounds like the merciful God of *Jonah* but can any God be merciful to a nation that does not repent of the evil it does? That makes, sells and uses what kills, cripples and warps even the unborn? Jesus learned from *Jonah*, *Micah* and *Nahum* what governments of Britain and the USA refuse to learn from Jesus. They act like Moses and Elijah, deliberately killing and diseasing thousands of civilians who cannot harm them. They do it without the old Hebrew excuse of being slaves wanting freedom or wanderers needing a homeland, without the Crusaders' excuse of defending a True Faith, without the Liberal excuse of spreading democracy. The one idea behind such war is that any number of foreigners can be killed to keep up global company profits, though politicians give nicer-sounding reasons. The inevitable victory of big arms-selling nations over small arms-buying ones has provoked counter-attacks. Just now these have killed very few, but enough to prove that this world ruled by greed is hatching one ruled by revenge. Old and New Testaments should teach us to reform our ways for our children's sake.

I belong to a small nation that for centuries has exported more soldiers and weapons than the defence of it ever needed. It now contains more destructive nuclear missiles and launching machines than any nation outside the USA. England has the good sense to contain hardly any. I hope the reform of Britain starts in Scotland.

jonah

Now the word of the Lord came unto Jonah the son of Amittai, saying, ²'Arise, go to Nineveh, that great city, and cry against it, for their wickedness is come up before me.' ³But Jonah rose up to flee unto Tarshish from the presence of the Lord, and went down to Joppa; and he found a ship going to Tarshish: so he paid the fare thereof, and went down into it, to go with them unto Tarshish from the presence of the Lord.

⁴But the Lord sent out a great wind into the sea, and there was a mighty tempest in the sea, so that the ship was like to be broken. ⁵Then the mariners were afraid, and cried every man unto his god, and cast forth the wares that were in the ship into the sea, to lighten it of them. But Jonah was gone down into the sides of the ship; and he lay, and was fast asleep. ⁶So the shipmaster came to him, and said unto him, 'What meanest thou, O sleeper? Arise, call upon thy God, if so be that God will think upon us, that we perish not.' ⁷And they said every one to his fellow, 'Come, and let us cast lots, that we may know for whose cause this evil is upon us.' So they cast lots, and the lot fell upon Jonah. ⁸Then said they unto him, 'Tell us, we pray thee, for whose cause this evil is upon us. What is thine occupation? And whence

comest thou? What is thy country? And of what people art thou?' ⁹And he said unto them, 'I am an Hebrew; and I fear the Lord, the God of heaven, which hath made the sea and the dry land.' ¹⁰Then were the men exceedingly afraid, and said unto him, 'Why hast thou done this?' For the men knew that he fled from the presence of the Lord, because he had told them.

¹¹Then said they unto him, 'What shall we do unto thee, that the sea may be calm unto us?' For the sea wrought, and was tempestuous. ¹²And he said unto them, 'Take me up, and cast me forth into the sea; so shall the sea be calm unto you: for I know that for my sake this great tempest is upon you.' ¹³Nevertheless the men rowed hard to bring it to the land; but they could not, for the sea wrought, and was tempestuous against them. ¹⁴Wherefore they cried unto the Lord, and said, 'We beseech thee, O Lord, we beseech thee, let us not perish for this man's life, and lay not upon us innocent blood: for thou, O Lord, hast done as it pleased thee.' ¹⁵So they took up Jonah, and cast him forth into the sea, and the sea ceased from her raging. ¹⁶Then the men feared the Lord exceedingly, and offered a sacrifice unto the Lord, and made vows.

¹⁷Now the Lord had prepared a great fish to swallow up Jonah. And Jonah was in the belly of the fish three days and three nights.

2 Then Jonah prayed unto the Lord his God out of the fish's belly, ²and said, 'I cried by reason of mine affliction

unto the Lord, and he heard me; out of the belly of hell cried I, and thou heardest my voice. ³ For thou hadst cast me into the deep, in the midst of the seas; and the floods compassed me about: all thy billows and thy waves passed over me. ⁴ Then I said, "I am cast out of thy sight; yet I will look again toward thy holy temple." ⁵ The waters compassed me about, even to the soul: the depth closed me round about, the weeds were wrapped about my head. ⁶ I went down to the bottoms of the mountains; the earth with her bars was about me for ever: yet hast thou brought up my life from corruption, O Lord my God. ⁷ When my soul fainted within me I remembered the Lord: and my prayer came in unto thee, into thine holy temple. ⁸ They that observe lying vanities forsake their own mercy. ⁹ But I will sacrifice unto thee with the voice of thanksgiving; I will pay that that I have vowed. Salvation is of the Lord.'

¹⁰ And the Lord spake unto the fish, and it vomited out Jonah upon the dry land.

3 And the word of the Lord came unto Jonah the second time, saying, ² 'Arise, go unto Nineveh, that great city, and preach unto it the preaching that I bid thee.' ³ So Jonah arose, and went unto Nineveh, according to the word of the Lord. Now Nineveh was an exceeding great city of three days' journey. ⁴ And Jonah began to enter into the city a day's journey, and he cried, and said, 'Yet forty days, and Nineveh shall be overthrown.'

⁵ So the people of Nineveh believed God, and proclaimed

a fast, and put on sackcloth, from the greatest of them even to the least of them. ⁶For word came unto the king of Nineveh, and he arose from his throne, and he laid his robe from him, and covered him with sackcloth, and sat in ashes. ⁷And he caused it to be proclaimed and published through Nineveh by the decree of the king and his nobles, saying, 'Let neither man nor beast, herd nor flock, taste any thing: let them not feed, nor drink water. ⁸But let man and beast be covered with sackcloth, and cry mightily unto God: yea, let them turn every one from his evil way, and from the violence that is in their hands. ⁹Who can tell if God will turn and repent, and turn away from his fierce anger, that we perish not?'

¹⁰And God saw their works, that they turned from their evil way; and God repented of the evil that he had said that he would do unto them; and he did it not.

4 But it displeased Jonah exceedingly, and he was very angry. ²And he prayed unto the Lord, and said, 'I pray thee, O Lord, was not this my saying, when I was yet in my country? Therefore I fled before unto Tarshish, for I knew that thou art a gracious God, and merciful, slow to anger, and of great kindness, and repentest thee of the evil. ³Therefore now, O Lord, take, I beseech thee, my life from me, for it is better for me to die than to live.'

⁴Then said the Lord, 'Doest thou well to be angry?' ⁵So Jonah went out of the city, and sat on the east side of the city, and there made him a booth, and sat under it in the shadow,

till he might see what would become of the city. ⁶And the Lord God prepared a gourd, and made it to come up over Jonah, that it might be a shadow over his head, to deliver him from his grief. So Jonah was exceeding glad of the gourd. ⁷But God prepared a worm when the morning rose the next day, and it smote the gourd that it withered. ⁸And it came to pass, when the sun did arise, that God prepared a vehement east wind; and the sun beat upon the head of Jonah, that he fainted, and wished in himself to die, and said, 'It is better for me to die than to live.' ⁹And God said to Jonah, 'Doest thou well to be angry for the gourd?' And he said, 'I do well to be angry, even unto death.' ¹⁰Then said the Lord, 'Thou hast had pity on the gourd, for the which thou hast not laboured, neither madest it grow; which came up in a night, and perished in a night. ¹¹And should not I spare Nineveh, that great city, wherein are more than sixscore thousand persons that cannot discern between their right hand and their left hand; and also much cattle?'

micah

The word of the Lord that came to Micah the Morasthite in the days of Jotham, Ahaz, and Hezekiah, kings of Judah, which he saw concerning Samaria and Jerusalem.

²Hear, all ye people; hearken, O earth,
    and all that therein is:
        and let the Lord God be witness against you,
        the Lord from his holy temple.
³For, behold, the Lord cometh forth
    out of his place,
        and will come down, and tread upon the high
        places of the earth.
⁴And the mountains shall be molten under him,
    and the valleys shall be cleft,
        as wax before the fire, and as the waters
        that are poured down a steep place.
⁵For the transgression of Jacob is all this,
    and for the sins of the house of Israel.
        What is the transgression of Jacob?
        Is it not Samaria?
        And what are the high places of Judah?
        Are they not Jerusalem?

⁶ Therefore I will make Samaria as an heap
    of the field, and as plantings of a vineyard:
        and I will pour down the stones thereof
    into the valley,
        and I will discover the foundations thereof.
⁷ And all the graven images thereof shall be
    beaten to pieces,
        and all the hires thereof shall be burned with
    the fire,
        and all the idols thereof will I lay desolate,
    for she gathered it of the hire of an harlot,
        and they shall return to the hire of an
    harlot.
⁸ Therefore I will wail and howl,
    I will go stripped and naked:
        I will make a wailing like the dragons,
    and mourning as the owls.
⁹ For her wound is incurable;
    for it is come unto Judah;
        he is come unto the gate of my people,
    even to Jerusalem.
¹⁰ Declare ye it not at Gath, weep ye not at all:
    in the house of Aphrah roll thyself in the dust.
¹¹ Pass ye away, thou inhabitant of Saphir,
    having thy shame naked:
        the inhabitant of Zaanan came not forth in the
    mourning of Beth-ezel;
        he shall receive of you his standing.

¹² For the inhabitant of Maroth waited carefully
for good, but evil came down from the Lord
unto the gate of Jerusalem.
¹³ O thou inhabitant of Lachish,
bind the chariot to the swift beast:
she is the beginning of the sin
to the daughter of Zion,
for the transgressions of Israel
were found in thee.
¹⁴ Therefore shalt thou give presents
to Moresheth-gath: the houses of Achzib
shall be a lie to the kings of Israel.
¹⁵ Yet will I bring an heir unto thee,
O inhabitant of Mareshah:
he shall come unto Adullam
the glory of Israel.
¹⁶ Make thee bald, and poll thee
for thy delicate children;
enlarge thy baldness as the eagle;
for they are gone into captivity from
thee.

2 Woe to them that devise iniquity,
and work evil upon their beds!
When the morning is light, they practise it,
because it is in the power of their
hand.

²And they covet fields, and take them by violence;
   and houses, and take them away,
      so they oppress a man and his house,
      even a man and his heritage.
³Therefore thus saith the Lord:
   Behold, against this family do I devise an evil,
      from which ye shall not remove your necks;
   neither shall ye go haughtily:
      for this time is evil.
⁴In that day shall one take up a parable against you,
   and lament with a doleful lamentation, and say,
      'We be utterly spoiled:
   he hath changed the portion of my people:
      how hath he removed it from me!
   Turning away he hath divided our fields.'
⁵Therefore thou shalt have none that shall cast
   a cord by lot in the congregation of the Lord.
⁶'Prophesy ye not,' say they to them that prophesy,
   they shall not prophesy to them,
      that they shall not take shame.'
⁷O thou that art named the house of Jacob,
   is the spirit of the Lord straitened?
      Are these his doings?
   Do not my words do good
      to him that walketh up-rightly?
⁸Even of late my people is risen up as an enemy:
   ye pull off the robe with the garment
      from them that pass by securely
   as men averse from war.

⁹ The women of my people have ye cast out
from their pleasant houses;
from their children have ye taken away
my glory for ever.
¹⁰Arise ye, and depart; for this is not your rest:
because it is polluted, it shall destroy you,
even with a sore destruction.
¹¹ If a man walking in the spirit and falsehood do lie,
saying, 'I will prophesy unto thee of wine
and of strong drink,' he shall even be
the prophet of this people.
¹² I will surely assemble, O Jacob, all of thee;
I will surely gather the remnant of Israel;
I will put them together as the sheep of
Bozrah,
as the flock in the midst of their fold:
they shall make great noise by reason of
the multitude of men.
¹³ The breaker is come up before them:
they have broken up, and have passed
through the gate, and are gone out by it:
and their king shall pass before them,
and the Lord on the head
of them.

3   And I said: Hear, I pray you, O heads of Jacob,
and ye princes of the house of Israel,
is it not for you to know judgment?

² Who hate the good, and love the evil;
   who pluck off their skin from off them,
   and their flesh from off their bones;
³ who also eat the flesh of my people,
   and flay their skin from off them;
      and they break their bones and chop them
   in pieces, as for the pot, and as flesh
      within the caldron.
⁴ Then shall they cry unto the Lord,
   but he will not hear them: he will even
      hide his face from them at that time,
   as they have behaved themselves ill
      in their doings.
⁵ Thus saith the Lord concerning the prophets
   that make my people err,
      that bite with their teeth, and cry, 'Peace';
   and he that putteth not into their mouths,
      they even prepare war against him.
⁶ Therefore night shall be unto you,
   that ye shall not have a vision;
      and it shall be dark unto you,
   that ye shall not divine;
      and the sun shall go down over the prophets,
   and the day shall be dark over them.
⁷ Then shall the seers be ashamed,
   and the diviners confounded: yea,
      they shall all cover their lips,
   for there is no answer of God.

⁸ But truly I am full of power by the spirit
of the Lord, and of judgment, and of might,
to declare unto Jacob his transgression,
and to Israel his sin.
⁹ Hear this, I pray you, ye heads of the house
of Jacob, and princes of the house of Israel,
that abhor judgment, and pervert all
equity.
¹⁰ They build up Zion with blood,
and Jerusalem with iniquity.
¹¹ The heads thereof judge for reward,
and the priests thereof teach for hire,
and the prophets thereof divine for money;
yet will they lean upon the Lord, and say,
'Is not the Lord among us?
None evil can come upon us.'
¹² Therefore shall Zion for your sake be plowed
as a field, and Jerusalem shall become heaps,
and the mountain of the house
as the high places of the
forest.

4
But in the last days it shall come to pass,
that the mountain of the house of the Lord
shall be established
in the top of the mountains,
and it shall be exalted above the hills;
and people shall flow unto it.

²And many nations shall come, and say, 'Come,
and let us go up to the mountain of the Lord,
and to the house of the God of Jacob;
and he will teach us of his ways,
and we will walk in his paths,'
for the law shall go forth of Zion,
and the word of the Lord from
Jerusalem.
³And he shall judge among many people, and
rebuke strong nations afar off;
and they shall beat their swords into plow-
shares,
and their spears into pruninghooks:
nation shall not lift up a sword against
nation,
neither shall they learn war any more.
⁴But they shall sit every man under his vine
and under his fig tree;
and none shall make them afraid;
for the mouth of the Lord of hosts hath
spoken it.
⁵For all people will walk every one in the name
of his god, and we will walk in the name
of the Lord our God for ever and ever.
⁶In that day, saith the Lord, will I assemble her
that halteth, and I will gather her
that is driven out, and her that I have
afflicted;

⁷and I will make her that halted a remnant,
  and her that was cast far off a strong nation;
    and the Lord shall reign over them
    in mount Zion from henceforth, even for ever.
⁸And thou, O tower of the flock, the
  strong hold of the daughter of Zion,
    unto thee shall it come, even the first
    dominion;
      the kingdom shall come to the daughter of
      Jerusalem.
⁹Now why dost thou cry out aloud?
  Is there no king in thee? Is thy counsellor
    perished?
  For pangs have taken thee as a woman in travail.
¹⁰Be in pain, and labour to bring forth,
  O daughter of Zion, like a woman in travail;
    for now shalt thou go forth out of the city,
  and thou shalt dwell in the field, and thou
    shalt go even to Babylon; there shalt thou
  be delivered; there the Lord shall redeem thee
    from the hand of thine enemies.
¹¹Now also many nations are gathered against thee,
  that say, 'Let her be defiled,
    and let our eye look upon Zion.'
¹²But they know not the thoughts of the Lord,
  neither understand they his counsel:
    for he shall gather them as the sheaves
    into the floor.

¹³Arise and thresh, O daughter of Zion,
for I will make thine horn iron,
and I will make thy hoofs brass;
and thou shalt beat in pieces many people,
and I will consecrate their gain unto the Lord,
and their substance unto the Lord
of the whole earth.

5 Now gather thyself in troops, O daughter of troops:
he hath laid siege against us: they shall smite
the judge of Israel with a rod upon
the cheek.
² But thou, Beth-lehem Ephratah, though thou be
little among the thousands of Judah,
yet out of thee shall he come forth unto me
that is to be ruler in Israel; whose goings forth
have been from of old, from
everlasting.
³ Therefore will he give them up, until the time
that she which travaileth hath brought forth;
then the remnant of his brethren shall return
unto the children of Israel.
⁴And he shall stand and feed in the strength
of the Lord, in the majesty of the name
of the Lord his God; and they shall abide;
for now shall he be great unto the ends of the
earth.

⁵And this man shall be the peace,
>   when the Assyrian shall come into our land:
>   and when he shall tread in our palaces,
>   then shall we raise against him seven shepherds,
>   and eight principal men.
⁶And they shall waste the land of Assyria
>   with the sword, and the land of Nimrod
>   in the entrances thereof:
>   thus shall he deliver us from the Assyrian,
>   when he cometh into our land,
>   and when he treadeth within our borders.
⁷And the remnant of Jacob shall be in the midst
>   of many people as a dew from the Lord,
>   as the showers upon the grass,
>   that tarrieth not for man,
>   nor waiteth for the sons of men.
⁸And the remnant of Jacob shall be
>   among the Gentiles in the midst of many people
>   as a lion among the beasts of the forest,
>   as a young lion among the flocks of sheep,
>   who, if he go through, both treadeth down,
>   and teareth in pieces, and none can deliver.
⁹Thine hand shall be lifted up
>   upon thine adversaries,
>   and all thine enemies shall be cut off.
¹⁰And it shall come to pass in that day, saith the Lord,
>   that I will cut off thy horses
>   out of the midst of thee,
>   and I will destroy thy chariots:

¹¹ and I will cut off the cities of thy land, and throw
down all thy strong holds:
¹² and I will cut off witchcrafts out of thine hand;
and thou shalt have no more soothsayers:
¹³ thy graven images also will I cut off,
and thy standing images out of the midst of thee;
and thou shalt no more worship the work
of thine hands.
¹⁴ And I will pluck up thy groves
out of the midst of thee:
so will I destroy thy cities.
¹⁵ And I will execute vengeance in anger and fury
upon the heathen, such as they have not heard.

6 Hear ye now what the Lord saith:
Arise, contend thou before the mountains,
and let the hills hear thy voice.
² Hear ye, O mountains, the Lord's controversy,
and ye strong foundations of the earth;
for the Lord hath a controversy with his
people,
and he will plead with Israel.
³ O my people, what have I done unto thee?
And wherein have I wearied thee?
Testify against me.
⁴ For I brought thee up out of the land of Egypt,
and redeemed thee out of the house of servants;
and I sent before thee Moses, Aaron,
and Miriam.

⁵ O my people, remember now what Balak
   king of Moab consulted, and what Balaam
the son of Beor answered him
   from Shittim unto Gilgal;
      that ye may know the righteousness of the
   Lord.
⁶ Wherewith shall I come before the Lord,
   and bow myself before the high God?
      Shall I come before him with burnt offerings,
   with calves of a year old?
⁷ Will the Lord be pleased with thousands of rams,
   or with ten thousands of rivers of oil?
      Shall I give my firstborn for my transgression,
   the fruit of my body for the sin of my soul?
⁸ He hath shewed thee, O man, what is good;
   and what doth the Lord require of thee,
      but to do justly, and to love mercy,
   and to walk humbly with thy God?
⁹ The Lord's voice crieth unto the city,
   and the man of wisdom shall see thy name:
      hear ye the rod, and who hath
   appointed it.
¹⁰ Are there yet the treasures of wickedness
   in the house of the wicked,
      and the scant measure that is
   abominable?
¹¹ Shall I count them pure with the wicked balances,
   and with the bag of deceitful weights?

¹² For the rich men thereof are full of violence,
and the inhabitants thereof have spoken lies
and their tongue is deceitful in
their mouth.
¹³ Therefore also will I make thee sick in smiting thee,
in making thee desolate because of thy sins.
¹⁴ Thou shalt eat, but not be satisfied;
and thy casting down
shall be in the midst of thee;
and thou shalt take hold, but shalt not deliver;
and that which thou deliverest
will I give up to the sword.
¹⁵ Thou shalt sow, but thou shalt not reap;
thou shalt tread the olives,
but thou shalt not anoint thee with oil;
and sweet wine, but shalt not drink wine.
¹⁶ For the statutes of Omri are kept,
and all the works of the house of Ahab,
and ye walk in their counsels,
that I should make thee a desolation,
and the inhabitants thereof an hissing:
therefore ye shall bear the reproach
of my people.

7 Woe is me! For I am as when they have gathered
the summer fruits, as the grapegleanings
of the vintage: there is no cluster to eat:
my soul desired the firstripe fruit.

² The good man is perished out of the earth,
  and there is none upright among men;
    they all lie in wait for blood;
  they hunt every man his brother with a net.
³ That they may do evil with both hands earnestly,
  the prince asketh, and the judge asketh
    for a reward; and the great man,
  he uttereth his mischievous desire:
    so they wrap it up.
⁴ The best of them is as a brier,
  the most upright is sharper than a thorn hedge:
    the day of thy watchmen
  and thy visitation cometh;
    now shall be their perplexity.
⁵ Trust ye not in a friend, put ye not confidence
  in a guide: keep the doors of thy mouth
    from her that lieth in thy bosom.
⁶ For the son dishonoureth the father,
  the daughter riseth up against her mother,
    the daughter in law against her
  mother in law;
    a man's enemies are the men
  of his own house.
⁷ Therefore I will look unto the Lord;
  I will wait for the God of my salvation:
    my God will hear me.
⁸ Rejoice not against me, O mine enemy:
  when I fall, I shall arise; when I sit in darkness,
    the Lord shall be a light unto me.

⁹ I will bear the indignation of the Lord,
  because I have sinned against him,
    until he plead my cause,
  and execute judgment for me:
    he will bring me forth to the light,
  and I shall behold his righteousness.
¹⁰ Then she that is mine enemy shall see it,
  and shame shall cover her which said unto me,
    'Where is the Lord thy God?'
  Mine eyes shall behold her:
    now shall she be trodden down
  as the mire of the streets.
¹¹ In the day that thy walls are to be built,
  in that day shall the decree be far
    removed.
¹² In that day also he shall come even to thee
  from Assyria, and from the fortified cities,
    and from the fortress even to the river,
  and from sea to sea,
    and from mountain to mountain.
¹³ Notwithstanding the land shall be desolate
  because of them that dwell therein,
    for the fruit of their doings.
¹⁴ Feed thy people with thy rod,
  the flock of thine heritage, which dwell solitarily
    in the wood, in the midst of Carmel:
  let them feed in Bashan and Gilead,
    as in the days of old.

¹⁵According to the days of thy coming out of the land
 of Egypt will I shew unto him marvellous things.
¹⁶ The nations shall see and be confounded
 at all their might:
  they shall lay their hand upon their mouth,
  their ears shall be deaf.
¹⁷ They shall lick the dust like a serpent,
 they shall move out of their holes
  like worms of the earth:
 they shall be afraid of the Lord our God,
  and shall fear because of thee.
¹⁸ Who is a God like unto thee,
 that pardoneth iniquity, and passeth by
  the transgression of the remnant of his
 heritage?
  He retaineth not his anger for ever,
  because he delighteth in mercy.
¹⁹ He will turn again, he will have compassion
 upon us; he will subdue our iniquities;
  and thou wilt cast all their sins
 into the depths of the sea.
²⁰ Thou wilt perform the truth to Jacob,
 and the mercy to Abraham,
  which thou hast sworn unto our fathers
 from the days of old.

nahum

The burden of Nineveh. The book of the vision of Nahum the Elkoshite.

> ² God is jealous, and the Lord revengeth;
>> the Lord revengeth, and is furious;
>>> the Lord will take vengeance on his
>> adversaries,
>>> and he reserveth wrath for his
>> enemies.
> ³ The Lord is slow to anger, and great in power,
>> and will not at all acquit the wicked:
>>> the Lord hath his way in the whirlwind
>> and in the storm,
>>> and the clouds are the dust of his feet.
> ⁴ He rebuketh the sea, and maketh it dry,
>> and drieth up all the rivers:
>>> Bashan languisheth, and Carmel,
>> and the flower of Lebanon languisheth.
> ⁵ The mountains quake at him, and the hills melt,
>> and the earth is burned at his presence,
>>> yea, the world, and all that dwell
>> therein.

[6] Who can stand before his indignation?
    And who can abide in the fierceness of his anger?
        His fury is poured out like fire,
        and the rocks are thrown down by him.
[7] The Lord is good, a strong hold
    in the day of trouble;
        and he knoweth them that trust in him.
[8] But with an overrunning flood he will make
    an utter end of the place thereof,
        and darkness shall pursue his enemies.
[9] What do ye imagine against the Lord?
    He will make an utter end:
        affliction shall not rise up the second time.
[10] For while they be folden together as thorns,
    and while they are drunken as drunkards,
        they shall be devoured as stubble
        fully dry.
[11] There is one come out of thee,
    that imagineth evil against the Lord,
        a wicked counsellor.
[12] Thus saith the Lord, 'Though they be quiet,
    and likewise many,
        yet thus shall they be cut down,
        when he shall pass through.
        Though I have afflicted thee,
        I will afflict thee no more.
[13] For now will I break his yoke from off thee,
    and will burst thy bonds in sunder.'

[14]And the Lord hath given a commandment
  concerning thee,
    that no more of thy name be sown;
  out of the house of thy gods will I cut off
    the graven image and the molten image:
  I will make thy grave, for thou
    art vile.
[15]Behold upon the mountains the feet of him
  that bringeth good tidings, that publisheth peace!
    O Judah, keep thy solemn feasts,
  perform thy vows, for the wicked shall no more
    pass through thee; he is utterly
  cut off.

2 He that dasheth in pieces is come up before thy face:
  keep the munition, watch the way,
    make thy loins strong, fortify thy power
  mightily.
[2]For the Lord hath turned away the excellency of Jacob,
  as the excellency of Israel,
    for the emptiers have emptied them out,
  and marred their vine branches.
[3]The shield of his mighty men is made red,
  the valiant men are in scarlet:
    the chariots shall be with flaming torches
  in the day of his preparation,
    and the fir trees shall be terribly
  shaken.

⁴ The chariots shall rage in the streets,
    they shall justle one against another
        in the broad ways: they shall seem like
torches,
        they shall run like the lightnings.
⁵ He shall recount his worthies:
    they shall stumble in their walk;
        they shall make haste to the wall thereof,
    and the defence shall be prepared.
⁶ The gates of the rivers shall be opened,
    and the palace shall be dissolved.
⁷ And Huzzab shall be led away captive,
    she shall be brought up, and her maids
        shall lead her as with the voice of doves,
    tabering upon their breasts.
⁸ But Nineveh is of old like a pool of water,
    yet they shall flee away. 'Stand, stand,'
        shall they cry; but none shall
    look back.
⁹ 'Take ye the spoil of silver, take the spoil of gold:
    for there is none end of the store and glory
        out of all the pleasant furniture.'
¹⁰ She is empty, and void, and waste:
    and the heart melteth,
        and the knees smite together,
    and much pain is in all loins,
        and the faces of them all gather
blackness.

¹¹ Where is the dwelling of the lions,
 and the feedingplace of the young lions,
  where the lion, even the old lion, walked,
 and the lion's whelp, and none made them
  afraid?
¹² The lion did tear in pieces enough for his whelps,
 and strangled for his lionesses,
  and filled his holes with prey,
 and his dens with ravin.
¹³ Behold, I am against thee, saith the Lord of hosts,
 and I will burn her chariots in the smoke,
  and the sword shall devour thy young lions:
 and I will cut off thy prey from the earth,
  and the voice of thy messengers
 shall no more be heard.

3 Woe to the bloody city!
  It is all full of lies and robbery;
   the prey departeth not.
² The noise of a whip, and the noise of the rattling of
 the wheels, and of the pransing horses,
  and of the jumping chariots.
³ The horseman lifteth up both the bright sword
 and the glittering spear:
  and there is a multitude of slain,
 and a great number of carcases;
  and there is none end of their corpses;
 they stumble upon their corpses:

⁴ because of the multitude of the whoredoms of
the wellfavoured harlot, the mistress of
witchcrafts,
that selleth nations through her whoredoms,
and families through her
witchcrafts.
⁵ Behold, I am against thee, saith the Lord of hosts;
and I will discover thy skirts upon thy face,
and I will shew the nations thy nakedness,
and the kingdoms thy shame.
⁶ And I will cast abominable filth upon thee,
and make thee vile,
and will set thee as a
gazingstock.
⁷ And it shall come to pass, that all they that look
upon thee shall flee from thee, and say,
'Nineveh is laid waste: who will bemoan
her?'
Whence shall I seek comforters
for thee?
⁸ Art thou better than populous No,
that was situate among the rivers,
that had the waters round about it,
whose rampart was the sea,
and her wall was from the sea?
⁹ Ethiopia and Egypt were her strength,
and it was infinite;
Put and Lubim were thy helpers.

¹⁰ Yet was she carried away, she went into captivity;
   her young children also were dashed in pieces
      at the top of all the streets;
   and they cast lots for her honourable men,
      and all her great men were bound in chains.
¹¹ Thou also shalt be drunken:
   thou shalt be hid, thou also shalt seek strength
      because of the enemy.
¹² All thy strong holds shall be like fig trees
   with the firstripe figs: if they be shaken,
      they shall even fall into the mouth of the
   eater.
¹³ Behold, thy people in the midst of thee are women:
   the gates of thy land shall be set wide open
      unto thine enemies:
   the fire shall devour thy bars.
¹⁴ Draw thee waters for the siege,
   fortify thy strong holds:
      go into clay, and tread the morter,
   make strong the brickkiln.
¹⁵ There shall the fire devour thee;
   the sword shall cut thee off, it shall eat thee up
      like the canker-worm:
   make thyself many as the canker-worm,
      make thyself many as the locusts.
¹⁶ Thou hast multiplied thy merchants above
   the stars of heaven: the canker-worm spoileth,
      and flieth away.

[17] Thy crowned are as the locusts, and thy captains
  as the great grasshoppers,
    which camp in the hedges in the cold day,
  but when the sun ariseth they flee away,
    and their place is not known where they are.
[18] Thy shepherds slumber, O king of Assyria:
  thy nobles shall dwell in the dust:
    thy people is scattered upon the mountains,
  and no man gathereth them.
[19] There is no healing of thy bruise;
  thy wound is grievous:
    all that hear the bruit of thee shall clap
  the hands over thee: for upon whom
    hath not thy wickedness passed continually?

the pocket canons

genesis – *introduced by steven rose*	£1.00 pbk
exodus – *introduced by david grossman*	£1.00 pbk
ruth – *introduced by joanna trollope*	£1.50 pbk
samuel – *introduced by meir shalev*	£1.50 pbk
job – *introduced by louis de bernières*	£1.00 pbk
psalms – *introduced by bono*	£1.50 pbk
proverbs – *introduced by charles johnson*	£1.00 pbk
ecclesiastes – *introduced by doris lessing*	£1.00 pbk
song of solomon – *introduced by a s byatt*	£1.00 pbk
isaiah – *introduced by peter ackroyd*	£1.50 pbk
jonah – *introduced by alasdair gray*	£1.50 pbk
wisdom – *introduced by piers paul read*	£1.50 pbk
matthew – *introduced by a n wilson*	£1.00 pbk
mark – *introduced by nick cave*	£1.00 pbk
luke – *introduced by richard holloway*	£1.00 pbk
john – *introduced by blake morrison*	£1.00 pbk
acts – *introduced by p d james*	£1.50 pbk
romans – *introduced by ruth rendell*	£1.50 pbk
corinthians – *introduced by fay weldon*	£1.00 pbk
hebrews – *introduced by karen armstrong*	£1.50 pbk
revelation – *introduced by will self*	£1.00 pbk

All of the above titles can be ordered directly from:
Canongate Books, 14 High Street, Edinburgh EH1 1TE
Tel 0131 557 5111   Fax 0131 557 5211